MW00656954

GALE
CENGAGE Learning

Drama for Students, Volume 2

McNeil, Gary Oudersluys, Maureen Richards, *Research Specialists*
Julia C. Daniel, Tamara C. Nott, Tracie A. Richardson, Cheryl L. Warnock, *Research Associates*

Susan M. Trosky, *Permissions Manager*
Kimberly F. Smilay, *Permissions Specialist*
Sarah Chesney, *Permissions Associate*
Steve Cusack, Kelly A. Quin, *Permissions Assistants*

Mary Beth Trimper, *Production Director*
Evi Seoud, *Assistant Production Manager*
Shanna Heilveil, *Production Assistant*

Randy Bassett, *Image Database Supervisor*
Mikal Ansari, Robert Duncan, *Imaging Specialists*
Pamela A. Reed, *Photography Coordinator*

Cynthia Baldwin, *Product Design Manager*
Cover design: Michelle DiMercurio, *Art Director*
Page design: Pamela A. E. Galbreath, *Senior Art Director*

Gale Research
835 Penobscot Building
645 Griswold St.
Detroit, MI 48226-4094

This book is printed on acid-free paper that meets the minimum requirements of American National Standard for Information Sciences—Permanence Paper for Printed Library Materials, ANSI Z39.48-1984.

ISBN 0-7876-1684-2

ISSN applied for and pending
Printed in the United States of America
10 9 8 7 6 5 4 3

The Miracle Worker

William Gibson

1957

Introduction

Initially written for television, *The Miracle Worker* by William Gibson first aired in 1957. After it was warmly received by television audiences, it was rewritten for the stage and opened on Broadway in 1959 at the Playhouse Theatre. Although some of the reviews were mixed, the audience response was very favorable and during its run the first production of *The Miracle Worker* rarely failed to fill the 1,000 seat theatre.

Drawing heavily from letters written by Anne Sullivan in 1887, as well as from Helen Keller's autobiography, William Gibson constructed a drama around the events that took place when Helen Keller and her teacher, Anne Sullivan, first met in the 1880s. The exchanges that take place in *The Miracle Worker* are all derived from factual events that Gibson has woven together to construct a fluid, emotionally real, depiction of the "miracle" Anne Sullivan was able to work: teaching Helen Keller language.

Audiences and critics alike were most drawn to *The Miracle Worker's* honest and emotionally vivid portrayal of the relationship between Annie (as she is called in the play) and Helen. The actors' intense energy and commitment to truth in the scenes of physical struggle between Annie and Helen were held as the most memorable moments of the play when it first opened on Broadway. Audiences found the story of Annie's struggle to teach Helen language and her eventual success life affirming and uplifting. Surrounding the major themes of change and transformation and language and meaning is basic integrity and emotional honesty. These two elements are the strongest reasons that *The Miracle Worker* is so popular among audiences and has been called an American Theatre classic.

Author Biography

William Gibson was born in the Bronx, New York, on November 13, 1914, the son of George Irving, a bank clerk, and Florence (Dore) Gibson. Gibson spent his childhood in New York City and eventually attended the City College of New York, where he studied from 1930 until 1932. After graduation, Gibson moved to Kansas, supporting himself as a piano teacher while pursuing his interest in theatre. It was in Topeka, Kansas, that Gibson had his earliest plays produced. Most of these early works were light comedies; two of them were later revised and restaged: *A Cry Of The Players* and *Dinny and the Witches,* both in 1948. Shortly after his time in Kansas, Gibson met a psychoanalyst named Margaret Brenman; the two were married on September 6, 1940, and eventually had two sons, Thomas and David.

Gibson's first major critical and popular success in New York was *Two for The Seesaw,* which opened on Broadway in 1958. He was praised for the play's brisk dialogue and the compassion with which he endowed the characters. However, it is Gibson's second Broadway production, *The Miracle Worker,* for which he is best known.

Gibson first became fascinated with Anne Sullivan and her triumph as Helen Keller's teacher while reading the letters that Anne Sullivan wrote in

1887 describing her experiences in the Keller household. It was these letters and also Nella Brady's biography, *Anne Sullivan Macy,* that inspired Gibson to write about Anne Sullivan's accomplishments. Gibson first attempted to write *The Miracle Worker* as a solo dance piece but wrote it as a television play for the series *Playhouse 90,* which was produced by CBS. After *The Miracle Worker* was warmly received when it aired on CBS on February 7, 1957, Gibson received offers to adapt it for stage and film. He decided to write it for the stage because he wished to have more artistic control over the production. Although it opened to mixed reviews, positive press and word-of-mouth led to *The Miracle Worker's* success on Broadway. *The Miracle Worker* was adapted as a feature-length film starring Anne Bancroft as Annie and Patty Duke as Helen in 1962, and was again produced for television in 1979 with Patty Duke playing the role of Annie and Melissa Gilbert as Helen.

After *The Miracle Worker,* Gibson continued to write for the theatre and became a member of the Dramatists Guild. However, after *Golden Boy* (1964), which was a musical adaptation of Clifford Odets's play of the same name, Gibson largely withdrew from the New York theatre scene. It was during this time in the 1960s and 1970s that he founded and became president of the Berkshire Theatre Festival in Stockbridge, Massachusetts. Gibson did return to the New York stage, however, during the 1980s; *The Monday after the Miracle,* his sequel to *The Miracle Worker* opened on Broadway on December 14, 1982, at the Eugene O'Neill

Theatre. *The Monday after The Miracle* was a much darker piece than its predecessor and garnered poor reviews and attendance; it closed after a short run. *The Miracle Worker* continues to be Gibson's best known work and is the drama on which his reputation rests.

Plot Summary

Act One

The Miracle Worker is set in the 1880s and begins at the Keller home in Tuscumbia, Alabama. It is night, and three adults stand around the lamplit crib of the infant Helen Keller: her parents, Kate and Captain Arthur Keller, and a doctor. They are discussing a serious ailment which Helen has just barely survived. While the Captain sees the doctor out, Kate makes the horrifying discovery that because of the illness, the child can no longer see nor hear. The next scene introduces Helen's Aunt Ev and unsympathetic half-brother James, and reveals that in the five-and-a-half years since the first scene Helen has become a willful, feral child, indulged in everything because denial brings tantrums and no one knows how to teach her decent behavior. The Captain and Kate argue about Helen, he saying that after so many doctors have failed it is a waste of money to hire more, while she is unwilling to give up. The Captain relents, and a desperate inquiry leads eventually to "a suitable governess" from Boston, a young woman named Annie Sullivan.

The next scene shows Annie in Boston, preparing to leave the Perkins Institute for the Blind, where as a patient she moved from blindness to partial vision. She is 20, stubborn, humorous, and haunted by the loss of her younger brother, Jimmie, who died after they were separated at an orphanage. Arriving in Alabama, Annie is met at the station by Kate and the sarcastic James. Kate is apprehensive because of Annie's youth, but Annie assures her that youthful energy will help in the task ahead, and says she has another asset as well: "I've been blind." The women begin to warm to each other. Back at the Keller home, Annie irks the Captain by refusing to let him take her suitcase. She meets Helen, and immediately makes Helen understand that the suitcase is to go "up." Together, Annie and Helen get it upstairs to Annie's room while Kate, appreciating what she has just seen, placates the Captain. Upstairs, Annie teaches Helen to hand-spell "doll" and "cake" to get each, then is outsmarted when Helen hits her in the face with the doll and runs out the door, locking Annie in. Unable to find the key, Annie must be humiliatingly "rescued" with a ladder brought to her window. After dinner, Annie finds Helen at her favorite place, the water pump in the yard. Thinking she is alone, Helen brings forth the "vanished" bedroom key from her mouth and gleefully drops it down the well. Annie smiles, with "great respect, humor, and acceptance of challenge," and enters the house, leaving Helen alone as the lights dim to end Act One.

Act Two

As Act Two begins, Helen is spilling and breaking things in Annie's room. Annie, using sign language, stubbornly spells the name of each broken item into Helen's hand. Entering, Kate asks Annie if this has any meaning for Helen. Annie says it will have none until Helen understands what a word—a name—is. Asked why she then persists in the silent struggle, Annie shows her resilience and humor by replying, "I like to hear myself talk!" Alone that night, Annie experiences one of her frequent memory-trips back to the orphanage, the crones who made life there hateful, and her forced and final parting with her brother.

At breakfast, Helen's improper behavior (she runs about the table, placing her hands on the others' food) sparks a confrontation between the Captain—whose practice is to ignore Helen so that the family (mainly him) can converse—and Annie, who insists that all such indulgence of Helen must stop. Annie asks to be left alone with Helen. There follows the longest and most famous onstage fight in American theatre, unresolved even after several scripted pages of battle because the lights change from the dining-room to the yard, where the family awaits the outcome. Eventually, Helen staggers from the house, bumps into her mother's knees, and clutches them. Then comes Annie, battered but smiling, to report her victory. Helen has eaten from her own plate. With a spoon. And folded her napkin.

The Captain, angry at Annie and her treatment of his daughter, wants to fire the young teacher but is persuaded by Kate and Aunt Ev to grant Annie's request to isolate herself and Helen in the garden house for an entire week. Annie's plan is to make Helen dependent upon her for everything, thus forcing Helen to communicate with her, thus opening the only way for her to truly become Helen's teacher. While the Kellers take Helen on a long drive so she won't know on returning that she is at home, the "Garden House" theatrically appears in the back yard before the eyes of the audience, through the use of lighting, props, and furniture. Helen throws a fit at being left alone with Annie, then subsides exhausted. She won't let Annie touch her, but Annie gets her curiosity by hand-spelling to a servant child, and communication is re-established. That done, Helen is put to bed, and a striking stage setting ends Act Two: each of the Kellers is picked out by a shaft of moonlight, listening as Annie sings a lullaby to the unhearing Helen.

Act Three

Act Three begins as the deadline for the end of the "Garden House" experiment approaches. Helen is clean and disciplined and has learned to hand-spell many words to get treats, but Annie frustratedly feels that she has accomplished little more than "fingergames—no meaning." Helen has gestures and concepts—she touches her cheek to signify her mother—but has yet to connect these with the movements of Annie's fingers in her palm. Annie begs for another week, but the Kellers, seeing the improvements but not the gap left to close, refuse. Annie insists on keeping Helen until six, the official deadline, but as the time dwindles we see the harrowing effect of the ordeal on Annie. Helen will not give or receive affection and shows no signs, even as Annie desperately spells more words into her hands, of moving past fingergames to the universe of language and communication. At the stroke of six, the Garden House disappears before our eyes, Kate claims Helen and carries her out of sight, and Annie, alone at the end of her struggle, remembers again the loss of Jimmie and repeats a line often heard in that connection, "God owes me a resurrection."

Returned to her family, Helen acts up at dinner, and the family indulges her despite their assurances to Annie that they would not. Helen throws a pitcher of water on Annie, and Annie grabs up Helen and the pitcher and stalks out, vowing to make Helen refill the pitcher. The Captain angrily rises to go out and fire Annie, but James, the sarcastic idler, shows he has understood Annie by going to the door and resolutely standing up to his father, who despite his anger is finally impressed with his son.

In the yard, Annie is forcing Helen to pump water, meanwhile spelling w-a-t-e-r into Helen's hand, and "Now," as Gibson says, "the miracle happens." Helen has the breakthrough Annie has prayed for, and runs around the yard touching, and learning from Annie the names of the pump, the stoop, the trellis, and more. Annie calls out, and the scene is joined by the Kellers, the servants, and their children. Helen learns to spell "Mother" and

"Papa," and the family kneels to her in tears. Then Helen gropes her way across the yard to Annie, to learn what her "name" is. Annie spells it to Helen, who spells it back: "Teacher." Helen shows the depth of the miracle of her understanding by getting from her mother the keys Annie had used to lock her out or in, and bringing and giving them to Annie. The onlookers withdraw, leaving Annie and Helen alone onstage. Annie, who had sworn never to love again after the loss of Jimmie, spells into Helen's hand, "I love Helen," adding verbally her last words to Jimmie: "Forever and ever." Then she and Helen, hand in hand, cross the yard to go in to dinner.

Characters

Anagnos (ah-nah-nyose)

Anagnos, described by Gibson as "a stocky bearded man," is Annie's counselor at the Perkins Institution for the Blind. It is Anagnos who places Annie in the Kellers's home as a governess for Helen. He is loving and kindly with Annie, but he can also be stern when necessary.

Annie

See Anne Sullivan

Aunt Ev

Aunt Ev is described by Gibson as "a benign visitor" who serves as a catalyst for the Kellers's first contact with the Perkins Institute. Aunt Ev is a talkative woman who often tries to be helpful, but who can be a bit intrusive. She sometimes oversteps her place as a visitor in the Keller household and at one point even threatens to take matters into her own hands.

Blind Girls

The "Blind Girls," who range in age from 8 to 17 years old, are the girls at the Perkins Institution with whom Annie has the closest relationship. Together they are like sisters: excited, lively, and loving. The youngest of the girls has difficulty accepting Annie's departure to the Kellers. When Annie is leaving, it is the Blind Girls who give her the smoked glasses that became Annie's trademark. They also give Annie a doll to give to Helen.

Doctor

The doctor opens the play with Helen's parents, Kate and Arthur. He is an elderly man who provides comforting words to Helen's parents after their child has just come out of a high fever caused by what the Doctor calls "acute congestion of the stomach and brain."

Keller

See Captain Arthur Keller

Captain Arthur Keller

Captain Keller is referred to by Gibson as "a hearty gentleman in his forties" and throughout the play displays die greatest measure of doubt in Annie's ability to teach his daughter. Keller is a newspaper publisher who possesses much power, both in the business world and in his own home. Nothing is done and no decisions are made in the Keller household without his consent. When Annie first arrives on the scene, Keller is extremely skeptical of her abilities, especially because of her young age. He is also not used to Annie's forthrightness and considers her to be rude and unladylike. Throughout *The Miracle Worker* Annie fights the constant battle to win Captain Keller's acceptance in order to keep her job, but she does not win his respect until after she has worked her "miracle" with Helen.

Helen Keller

Helen, the recipient of the miracle that is worked in the play, is the six-and-a-half year old daughter of Kate and Arthur who is left deaf and blind after a serious illness as an infant. Her struggle to communicate and relate to the world around her necessitates the arrival of Annie to the Keller household. Despite her handicaps, Helen is a girl of exceptional intellect and cleverness, but it is her lack of restraint that leaves her thrashing around the world in which she lives without any focus or discipline. During the action of the play, the emphasis is mostly on Helen's battle of wills with Annie. Annie tries to get Helen to connect the hand symbols that she teaches her with the world around her. At the climax of the play, this connection is finally made with a substance that Helen remembers from a time in her infancy prior to her illness, namely water.

James Keller

James, Captain Keller's son from a previous marriage, is described by Gibson as "an indolent young man." James is often flippant and sarcastic, largely due to his inner turmoil. With all of the attention being paid to Helen and the baby, James is easily hurt and wears this hurt openly. When Annie arrives he is at first skeptical but eventually becomes one of her strongest supporters. This support reveals itself as important in Annie's struggle to prove to Captain Keller that she is a capable teacher.

Kate Keller

Defined at the play's beginning as "a young gentlewoman with a sweet girlish face," Kate Keller develops into a woman consumed with guilt over her daughter Helen's condition. She is patient and gentle with Helen, but when Annie arrives Kate must learn that it is sometimes necessary to use force while trying to teach her daughter. At first Kate has a difficult time letting Annie take control of Helen's discipline, but after witnessing Annie's success with Helen in two short weeks at the Keller household, Kate realizes that she must let go, relying upon her strength to help her do the best thing for her child.

Martha

Martha, a young African-American child, is playful and curious, and can also be a bit bossy, especially with Percy. In the scenes that she shares with Helen, Martha is both amazed and terrified by Helen's behavior.

Media Adaptations

- *The Miracle Worker* was originally written for television and produced on CBS's *Playhouse 90* in February of 1957. Teresa Wright starred as Annie and Patty McCormack portrayed Helen.
- The film version of *The Miracle Worker* was produced in 1962 by Metro-Goldwyn-Mayer. It was adapted by Gibson himself, directed by Arthur Penn, and stars Anne Bancroft as Annie and Patty Duke as Helen—both leads in the original Broadway production of the play. The film is available on videocassette.
- The 1979 television remake of *The Miracle Worker,* which stars Patty

Duke as the teacher Annie and Melissa Gilbert as Helen, is available on videocassette from Warner Home Video. The production bears noting, as the same script used for the original *Playhouse 90* production was used for this remake.

Offstage Voices

The "Offstage Voices" in *The Miracle Worker* serve different functions at different times in the play, but they are always directly related to Annie and her struggle. One of the recurring voices is "Boy's Voice," which is the voice of Annie's dead younger brother, Jimmie. This voice, along with the others, represents Annie's internal struggle with feelings of guilt, her motivation to succeed with Helen, and her will to continue living her own life.

Percy

Percy is a young African-American child who seems to be a bit younger than Martha. Although Percy is frightened of Helen, he becomes directly involved in Helen's education while he is staying in die garden house with Annie and Helen.

Servant

An African-American man who is a servant who helps with some of the heaviest labor around the Keller household. This servant has no lines in the play, and serves mainly to help change the set and move the large and weighty items that Viney, Percy, and Martha cannot move themselves.

Annie Sullivan

Annie Sullivan is the “miracle worker” to which the title of the play refers. She first appears while she is still at the Perkins Institution for the Blind, where she has lived as a pupil since she was a child. Everything that she has learned, including the sign language that she later uses with Helen, she has learned at Perkins. When Anagnos asks her to become Helen’s governess, as requested by the Keller family, it is her first job. At the age of twenty, Annie takes her first step out of the Perkins Institution and into her adult life. From the first moment that she enters the Keller household, Annie is met with skepticism and doubt, mostly because of her young age and lack of experience. This, however, does not deter her from what she feels must be done. When Annie and Helen first meet, Helen is a spoiled child who, because of her family’s pity, is allowed to do whatever she pleases. Annie’s first challenge is simply to get her to respond to discipline. After that, her time is devoted to teaching Helen hand symbols in the hope that she will eventually connect them with the objects and people around her, and thus learn “language.”

The other characters in the play also offer their own challenges to Annie. Captain Keller almost fires Annie because of what he calls her "Yankee" attitude, and they are constantly at odds with each other over the way that she treats Helen. It is only through clever manipulation that Annie is able to bide time until she can successfully prove herself to him. James Keller, in his usual sarcastic way, finds Annie's methods laughable at first, but he is eventually won over. Kate Keller also meets Annie with skepticism, but she is in such pain over Helen's condition that she is willing to let Annie have whatever she needs in order for Helen to have a better life.

The character who has the most direct effect on Annie throughout the play, however, is her own conscience, represented by the Offstage Voices. These voices represent Annie's past experiences and give her the motivation that she needs to succeed with Helen. Alone, these voices present the only direct threat to Annie's confidence and strong will. The most powerful of them all is the voice of her younger brother, Jimmie, whose death Annie blames on herself. Annie is not able to silence his voice until the end of the play, when the "miracle" finally happens and she clutches Helen to her promising to love her "forever and ever," just as she once promised Jimmie.

Viney

Viney, an African-American woman, is a

servant in charge of the daily housework and meals in the Keller household. She is cheerful, practical, and very adept at her job. Viney is also very loving and protective with the Keller children, and although Mildred, the Kellers's baby, is obviously her favorite, she appears to love Helen very much. It is difficult for Viney to know what to do with Helen and how to communicate with her.

Themes

In simplest terms, *The Miracle Worker* is the story of how one person can enter the lives of others and change them forever. During the course of the play, Annie Sullivan enters the Keller household and through her work to teach Helen—who is deaf, mute, and blind—language, ends up changing all of the characters's perceptions of the world, as well as changing her own world-view. By the end of the play the "miracle" that she works, teaching Helen language, has a direct effect on everyone's life and the way in which they live it.

Change and Transformation

The first overriding theme of *The Miracle Worker* is that of change and transformation. The characters of the play very much want to change their lives but are unsure of the extent to which they are willing to transform themselves. When Annie first comes to the Keller household to help with Helen, the Kellers are desperate for any change in their relationship with Helen. Once Annie begins to take charge of the situation, however, she meets with resistance. Mr. Keller is unaccustomed to her brash manner and is reluctant to give her control of Helen, while Kate finds it difficult to watch someone else take charge of her daughter's discipline. Annie is a very stubborn woman who does not give up easily and is able to manipulate both parents into letting her have the chance to prove herself; however, she must fight tooth and nail for this privilege again and again throughout the course of the play.

Topics for Further Study

- Discuss the use of food and drink as significant parts of the action of *The Miracle Worker*.
- The end of *The Miracle Worker* has been described by some critics as "too sentimental." Do you agree? What, then, does "sentimental" mean?
- Read *Two for the Seesaw*. What are the qualities of Anne Bancroft as an actress that would prompt directors to cast her as the heroine of two such different plays as *The Miracle*

Worker and *Two for the Seesaw?*

- How many kinds of sign language are used in the U. S.? Research the methods of hand-spelling used with people who are both deaf and blind

---

Throughout the play small changes are made within the lives of the characters, but the true transformation does not occur until the climax of the play when the "miracle" takes place. It is when Helen finally connects the simple hand symbols that Annie has been teaching her with actual objects and people that everything else falls into place. Helen's is utterly changed as she rushes around asking Annie the names of different objects and people. Mr. Keller and Kate finally realize the significance of Annie's methods and are able to believe in what can be done. It is also during this last scene that Kate is finally, after a difficult struggle, able to give Helen to Annie. Gibson describes this in the play's stage directions as "a moment in which [Kate] simultaneously finds and loses a child." Annie's transformation is complete when she can no longer hear the voices of her past haunting her; Annie then realizes that she can devote herself to loving and teaching Helen without and fear or doubt.

Language and Meaning

It is during the climactic scene at the end of Act Three that the second major theme, language and meaning, is resolved. The importancc of language is first emphasized in an early scene between Kate and Annie, shortly after Annie's arrival. Kate begins by asking Annie what she plans to teach Helen and Annie answers, "First, last, and —in between, language. . . . Language is to the mind more than light is to the eye." Annie is actually quoting someone else's words at this point, but it is obvious that she realized the significance of it because she was once blind herself and has benefitted from the language that she has learned. The question for Annie is how and whether it is possible to teach Helen language and its meaning.

In the beginning, the work that Annie does with Helen is simply a matter of discipline and repetition. Annie must first struggle to control Helen's extremely strong will, which had never been challenged prior to Annie's arrival. Once Annie begins to have progress in this area she is able to begin teaching Helen hand symbols for different objects. The hand symbols, at first, are just a repetition game to Helen, who does not make any connection between symbol and object; Annie hopes that through this repetition Helen will eventually start to connect the symbols with actual objects in her world. Annie's doubts about whether this method will work, however, are strong and eventually Annie realizes that it is necessary for Helen to depend on her for everything; only then will Helen be motivated to use the symbols that Annie teaches her. Annie convinces the Kellers to give her complete control over Helen and she then uses every method from repetition to force to resentment to keep Helen interested in learning. Annie's methods hold Helen's interest, but Annie expresses her realization of their inadequacy when she tells Helen: "Now all I have to teach you is—one word. Everything."

The final connection between language and meaning does come, but not until it seems that all the work that Annie has been in vain. After living secluded in the garden house for two weeks with Helen and Percy, Annie has no choice but to let Helen go back to the Kellers. In a short scene at the dinner table, Helen begins to recede back into her old ways. Annie will have none of it, and in a final battle of wills with Helen over spilled water, she inadvertently helps Helen make mat huge leap of connecting language to the world around her. In the triumphant scene at the water pump, Annie can finally exclaim about Helen that "She knows!" It is during this one scene that the themes of change and transformation and language and meaning come together in a demonstration of the power of love and determination and the strength of the human will.

Style

Flashback

The most striking aspect of the construction of *The Miracle Worker* is the style in which the play is written. Although realistic in tone, *The Miracle Worker* often makes use of cinematic shifts in time and space to illuminate the effect of the past on the present in a manner analogous to Arthur Miller's *Death Of A Salesman*. It is clear that Gibson was influenced by *Death Of A Salesman,* which was written in 1949, especially in terms of his use of flashback and stage space. The realistic tone of *The Miracle Worker* comes through in the dialogue, which is similar to the way that people talk to each other in real life. It is Gibson's use of flashback that brings about many of the cinematic shifts within the linear action of the play. The first of these flashback scenes occurs at the play's opening, when the audience learns how Helen Keller first became deaf and blind. The scene depicts the incident which sets the wheels in motion for the rest of the events in the play. Right after this scene, the audience is taken into "real" time and the action proceeds chronologically.

After this initial scene, the use of flashback in *The Miracle Worker* changes. Unlike *Death Of A Salesman,* in which the characters actually step into the past and play out scenes, Gibson uses offstage voices whenever he wants to set past events against the action of the present. Gibson uses this device solely with the main character, the miracle worker herself, Annie Sullivan. These voices from the past help the audience to understand why Annie does the things that she does while working with Helen in the Keller home. By using these voices, the audience is able to hear and see into Annie's mind. These moments are also the only time that the point of view of the play changes. Most of the time, as in most plays, the action unfolds before the audience's eyes as it happens and not through any particular character. However, in the flashback scenes in which Gibson uses offstage voices, the point of view changes because the audience is getting a glimpse of the past through the mind of Annie Sullivan.

Setting and Use of Space

The cinematic style that Gibson uses also can be seen with the setting of the play and the use of stage space. Gibson's use of stage space is also very similar to Arthur Miller's in *Death Of A Salesman.* Both playwrights establish a particular setting as a base for reality in their plays, in which only the basics are used. In *The Miracle Worker,* Gibson uses only the items that are actually used during the action of the play to establish the Kellers's home, such as the water pump and doors with locks. Anything that is not actually used by the characters in the play should only be suggested. Both playwrights use this particular technique so that the characters can enter into other areas of the play without having to do complicated set changes that would ruin the fluid motion of the play. As Gibson states in the script: "The convention of the staging is one of cutting through time and place, and its essential qualities are fluidity and spatial counterpoint." By using this convention, the audience is quickly taken from the Keller home to the Perkins Institution for the Blind, the train station, or the garden house, without disturbing the action of the play.

With the use of this staging convention, characters occupying different areas of the stage can affect one another. This can be seen early in the play when Annie is at the Perkins Institution where she is preparing to leave to go to the Keller home. In the scene, Annie is hearing the offstage voices of her past when Anagnos calls out her name, quickly bringing her back to the present. At this point, Annie answers him by calling out "Coming!" At the same moment, Kate, who is in the Keller home, catches the word "coming" and "stands half turned and attentive to it, almost as though hearing it." This is a prime example of how Gibson uses the space of the stage to bring worlds in the play together in order to show the effects that they have on each other. In production, the careful use of lighting helps to make these shifts in setting clear to the audience, as if a world is unfolding before their eyes instead of the action being interrupted for a change of set. This keeps the audience involved and helps to make them a part of the world of the play, which is similar to the way film directors use crossfades and other editing devices to manipulate their audience's attention.

Honesty

Although the cinematic style that Gibson uses in *The Miracle Worker* works very well, it is important to note that Gibson placed great importance on the play truthfulness. No matter what devices Gibson used in *The Miracle Worker,* honesty is apparent in his technique. Without honesty, whether dealing with the characters' relationships or the dramatic conflicts that arise in the action of the play, the audience will not connect with the play. It is due to the play's honesty that Gibson is able to use flashback, cinematic shifts, and other devices in order to inspire the audience and pull them into the world of Annie Sullivan and Helen Keller. The audience is able to believe in and care about what is happening in the world of the play because of the honesty with which Gibson endows every character and situation in *The Miracle Worker.*

Historical Context

Prejudice and Fear in America during the 1880s and 1950s

The Miracle Worker was written in the United States during the late 1950s, which was the beginning of a period of change in American society. The country had just witnessed the paranoia of the McCarthy hearings, during which many theatre artists were charged with participating in "un-American" activities, or simply accused of being Communists. The mid-to late 1950s also witnessed the beginning of the Civil Rights movement in the southern U.S., including in Alabama, where *The Miracle Worker* is set. In American theatre, audiences had seen the crumbling facade of the American dream in the plays of Tennessee Williams and Arthur Miller. All of these aspects are a part of *The Miracle Worker* in its form, origin, and focus.

Although the subject of *The Miracle Worker* is not the paranoia of possible Communist invasion or the civil rights of African Americans in the 1950s, both of these factor into an underlying theme of the play: prejudice and fear. In the play, the prejudice and fear that arise from misunderstanding are brought to light. The most obvious example of this is the way in which the Kellers treat Helen. They use Helen's handicap as a reason to treat her with pity and for their reluctance to discipline her. The Kellers's fear and ignorance of Helen's condition cause them to underestimate Helen's intelligence, and allow them to treat her like an animal.

Compare & Contrast

- **1880s:** Alabama and the rest of the South just finished living through the period of Reconstruction (1865-77) which followed the Civil War. Southerners were suspicious of the North's methods and ideas, including rights for African Americans.

  1950s: Alabama attracts international attention as the birthplace of the Civil Rights Movement. The Southern Christian Leadership Conference (SCLC), led by Martin Luther King, Jr., helped the black community to mobilize and plan a strategy to realize their goals, which included desegregation and voting rights.

  Today: The United States government and much of American society has adapted to accommodate and promote the ideas of Martin Luther King, Jr. and the Civil Rights Movement. There are still some citizens, however, who choose to keep their racist and separatists beliefs even though the law does not support them. Subversive groups such as the Ku Klux Klan continue to exist and promote their message of hatred and division.

- **1880s:** African Americans in the South struggle to find their place in society. Most work as servants in the households of the wealthy white families.
  1950s: The practice of segregation led to little opportunity for African Americans to receive higher education and advance to well-paying careers.
  Today: African Americans hold positions at all levels of business in the U.S. Nevertheless, racism continues to be a problem in American society. Great steps have been taken since the dawning of the Civil Rights Movement, but much is left to be done to lessen the racial problems in the United States.

- **1880s:** Sign language, like the hand symbols that Annie uses in *The Miracle Worker,* is introduced to American society. It is met with strong resistance and nongesticulating schools continue to hold prominence.

1950s: The invention of the tellatouch enables a sighted caller to communicate with a deaf-blind person who can read braille.
Today: More technological advances continue to be developed to help the visually and hearing impaired communicate effectively within a hearing and sighted society.

- **1880s:** Almshouses or asylums are used to house America's outcasts and disabled where they are used for forced labor to help defray maintenance costs. The Perkins Institution for the Blind (founded by Dr. Samuel Gridley Howe in 1832) continues to offer an alternative to asylums, as well as teaching the visually and hearing impaired.
  1950s: Blind and deaf students attend public schools with non-disabled students. Special day and residential schools are also common and continue to receive funding to help meet the needs of deaf and blind students as well as their teachers.
  Today: The Americans with Disabilities Act was passed in 1990 to address the needs of the disabled, from education and employment to telecommunications and public services.

Prejudice is also clearly present in the relationships that Captain Keller has with Annie and Viney. *The Miracle Worker* is set in the southern U.S. in the 1880s, shortly after the Reconstruction following the Civil War. During this period, the South resented the North's methods and ideas, especially those concerning the treatment and rights of former slaves. This view is dramatized in the play with the relationship Captain Keller has with Viney; he is very short with Viney, and does not appreciate when she offers her opinion of the changing circumstances in the Keller household after Annie's arrival. Viney displays a fear of Captain Keller and is unsure of her place in their relationship. The suspicion and resentment of the North by the South is seen in *The Miracle Worker* with the arrival of Annie, who is from the North and her relationship with Captain Keller. From the beginning, Captain Keller establishes himself as a man of the South while he is discussing the Battle of Vicksburg with his son James during Annie's first breakfast with the Kellers. The Battle of Vicksburg lasted for 47 days and ended with the victory of the North, led by Ulysses S. Grant, on July 4, 1863. Grant became famous for his ruthless determination during this Civil War battle and Captain Keller later compares Annie's stubbornness with Grant's. Captain Keller's prejudice and resentment can be seen in his remarks about Grant's drunkenness; therefore, his comparison of Annie and Grant can be construed as negative. Captain

Keller is also fearful of Annie's methods because of her young age and the fact that she herself is virtually blind. In these examples, Gibson is displaying deeply rooted prejudices common among many Americans.

American Theatre in the 1950s

During the 1950s, the American theatre saw many plays dealing with the problems of American society and the disenchantment that people sometimes experienced while trying to pursue the "American Dream." Arthur Miller's *Death Of A Salesman* (1949) is often considered a modern tragedy because of the depth of one simple man's struggle in American society. This play in particular had an effect upon the theatre structure and form of *The Miracle Worker*. In his play, Gibson uses flashback and past events to punctuate the action that is unfolding on stage in "real" time, as the audience is watching. Other artistic trends such as the use of psychological truth as a basis for the characters' conflicts and motivation were seen in plays like Tennessee Williams's *A Streetcar Named Desire* (1947). Gibson follows this trend as well in his use of offstage voices in *The Miracle Worker,* which represent Annie's subconscious and give her the motivation to do the difficult things that she does. By the end of the 1950s, however, these trends began to fade away as plays began to take nonrealistic and existential paths; an example of which is *Waiting For Godot* by Samuel Beckett.

The late 1950s were a difficult time in the U.S. for many people. Fear and prejudice were relevant themes in many aspects of American life, especially in the South. Some people were reluctant to change and desperately tried to hold on to their idea of American society, while others around them cried out for their own place in the world while expressing their views of what American society should be. Eventually, many Americans allowed change to enter their lives and like the Kellers in *The Miracle Worker* learned and grew together in the process.

Critical Overview

When *The Miracle Worker* first opened on Broadway on October 19, 1959, it was an instant popular success. Despite mixed reviews from the press, it had no trouble attracting 1,000 theatergoers a night during the length of its run. *The Miracle Worker* was William Gibson's second play to be produced on Broadway, and because of its success with the public, it is also the play for which he is best known and the one on which his reputation as a playwright rests.

The positive critiques of *The Miracle Worker* focus mostly on Gibson's honest and unsentimental treatment of the relationship between Helen and Annie. Gibson is praised for the wit and humor that he brings to the situation, and for the emotional purity with which he endows the struggle to bring Helen into the world around her by teaching her language. Much has been written about the acting out of the play's youthfulness and vigor by Anne Bancroft, who played Annie Sullivan, and Patty Duke, who played Helen Keller. Both of these actors were praised for the concentration, stamina, and passion that they brought to the play, especially during the now famous struggle between the two of them in the dining room. Next to the climactic scene by the water pump at the end of the play, this scene in the dining room is the one that critics and theatergoers remember most vividly. The pure, raw emotional energy of this moment in the play can, as critic Richard A. Duprey maintained, "work marvelous things in the soul." It is this emotional connection with the audience that kept the play well attended during its Broadway run and is largely why it continues to be produced today.

Most of the negative criticism that *The Miracle Worker* received was concerning the structure of the play itself. Critics expressed that what was characterized as an uneven and clumsy structure was a result of the play's adaptation from a television script. Some critics went as far as to say that Gibson sometimes confuses play writing with psychological counseling and although emotionally rewarding, *The Miracle Worker* is a less than perfect drama. Gibson's use of offstage voices came under fire from some critics as well. These criticisms of the structure of the play, however, never seem to come without praise of other areas of Gibson's talent. In Richard Hayes's review of *The Miracle Worker* in *Commonweal,* he praised the play's "affirmations of the human spirit," but declared: "One recognizes the content of the moment, of the experience, but is released into nothing else: essentially, it is a *fact* to which one has responded. That the fact may be a gratifying demonstration of human worth is, in itself, aesthetically irrelevant." Other critics echoed Hayes's sentiments, arguing that although it offers an emotionally satisfying night of theatre, *The Miracle Worker* does little to further the artistic development of drama as a genre.

Overall, the popular success and positive

criticism of *The Miracle Worker* have continued to eclipse the negative criticism that it has received, and have helped establish its reputation as a classic American play and one of the most life-affirming dramatic works to come out of the 1950s. Robert Brustein summed up Gibson's positive reputation when he observed in the *New Republic* that "Gibson possesses substantial literary and dramatic gifts and an integrity of the highest order. In addition, he brings to his works authentic compassion, wit, bite and humor, and a lively, literate prose style equaled by few American dramatists."

What Do I Read Next?

- *The Story of My Life,* by Helen Keller. Learn what this miracle worker accomplished.
- *Anne Sullivan Macy,* by Nella Brady. A fascinating account of Sullivan's life, and an examination

of what happens to a lifc that climaxes at the age of twenty-one.

- *The Seesaw Log,* by William Gibson. This the author's own account of the entire process of getting *Two for the Seesaw* produced on Broadway. There is not to be found a funnier or more truthful book about the farce, the frustrations, and the sheer lunacy of big-time commercial play production.
- *The Joy of Signing,* by Lottie L. Riekehof. An illustrated guide to sign language that provides a working understanding of the language of the deaf.

Further Reading

Atkinson, Brooks. "*Miracle Worker:* Two Strong Minds and Two Strong Players" in die *New York Times,* November 1, 1959, p. 1.

A favorable review of the play's Broadway premiere. Atkinson finds favor with both Gibson's material and the performances of the lead actresses.

Contemporary Literary Criticism, Volume 23, Gale, 1983.

Provides an overview of Gibson's work, providing criticism on a number of his plays, including *The Miracle Worker*.

Dictionary of Literary Biography, Volume 7: *Twentieth Century American Dramatists,* Gale, 1981.

An overview of Gibson's career, with insights into a number of his works.

Tynan, Kenneth. "Ireland Unvanquished" in the *New Yorker,* Vol. XXXV, no. 37, October 31, 1959, pp. 131-36.

A mixed review of *The Miracle Worker* that ultimately finds the play somewhat exploitive.

Sources

Brustein, Robert. "Two for the Miracle," in *The New Republic,* Vol. 144, no. 19, November 9, 1959, pp. 28-29.

Duprey, Richard A. "An Enema for the People" in his *Just Off the Aisle: The Ramblings of a Catholic Critic,* Newman Press, 1962, pp. 135-46.

Hayes, Richard. "Images" in *Commonweal,* Vol. LXXI, no. 10, December 4, 1959, p. 289.

CPSIA information can be obtained
at www.ICGtesting.com
Printed in the USA
BVHW041721071019
560429BV00030B/1676/P

9 781375 392525